Nostalgia, My Enemy

تَحَقُّق

قد كنتُ أنذرُ
يا ما كنتُ آملُ
والخريفُ يُلوِّنُ الغاباتِ بالذهبِ ،
وبالجوزيَّةِ
أو بالقرمز المكتوم ...
يا ما كنتُ آملُ أن أرى وجهَ العراقِ ضُحىً
وأن أرضى ضفائرَه الحياةُ علَيَّ ،
أن أُرضي عراكَ مائِه بالدمع مِلحاً
أن أطوفَ في شطوطِ أبي الخصيبِ ، لأسأل الأشجارَ :
هل تعرفنَ يا أشجارُ أنّى كان قبرُ أبي ؟
. . . .
. . . .

ويا ما كنتُ آملُ !

خلِّها ...
حلَّ الربيعُ يُتِمُّ دورتَه
فأشجارُ العراقِ تظل عاريةً
وأشجارُ العراقِ تظل عاليةً
وأشجارُ العراقِ ، وأنيسُها في السرِّ وجهُ أبي ...

London 21.05.2003

Nostalgia, My Enemy

Poems

~

SAADI YOUSSEF

Translated from the Arabic by
Sinan Antoon and Peter Money

GRAYWOLF PRESS

Grateful acknowledgment is made to *Across Borders, Banipal, Jadaliyya,* and
Washington Square for publishing early versions of poems in this collection.

This publication is made possible in part by a grant provided by the Minnesota
State Arts Board, through an appropriation by the Minnesota State Legislature
from the Minnesota general fund and its arts and cultural heritage fund with
money from the vote of the people of Minnesota on November 4, 2008, and a
grant from the Wells Fargo Foundation Minnesota. Significant support has also
been provided by the National Endowment for the Arts; Target; the McKnight
Foundation; and other generous contributions from foundations, corporations,
and individuals. To these organizations and individuals we offer our heartfelt
thanks.

Published by Graywolf Press
250 Third Avenue North, Suite 600
Minneapolis, Minnesota 55401

www.graywolfpress.org

Published in the United States of America

ISBN 978-1-55597-629-3

2 4 6 8 9 7 5 3 1
First Graywolf Printing, 2012

Library of Congress Control Number: 2012936230

Cover design: Kyle G. Hunter

Cover photo: Saadi Youssef. © Koutaiba Al-Janabi.

Frontispiece: "Fulfillment" in Saadi Youssef's own handwriting, in the Arabic
original.

Contents

Introduction

Saadi Youssef was born near Basra in 1934 and published his first collection in Iraq in 1952. In the six decades since, he has become one of the greatest living poets writing in Arabic. His prolific output—a staggering and remarkably diverse body of forty-six collections to date, let alone numerous translations of Whitman, Cavafy, Ritsos, Ungaretti, and Popa, among others—has influenced generations of Arab poets and shaped the trajectory of modern Arabic poetry. The late Mahmoud Darwish (1941–2008), the towering figure of Arabic poetry and culture, considered Youssef a major influence on his own work.

Youssef's "poetography" is, of course, intertwined with his biography and the tumultuous history of his country and the region. When he was still a teenager Iraq itself was a nascent nation-state on its way to genuine independence after toppling the pro-British monarchy to become a republic. Youssef was politicized at an early age and joined the Iraqi Communist Party like so many writers, poets, and fellow citizens of his generation. A commitment to and engagement in politics meant being subjected to many dangers and violent displacements. Youssef experienced prison and a series of exiles, the last of which has yet to end. He has had to watch in agony, from afar, his homeland be invaded by Anglo-American armies in 2003 and later disintegrate in civil war and sectarian violence. The rupture caused by the invasion and occupation of Iraq is impossible to overestimate. It has decimated an entire society, killing hundreds of thousands and displacing a few million Iraqis who live as refugees in neighboring countries. All of this and the compounded effects of dictatorship and genocidal sanctions (1991–2003) have scarred Iraqi collective memory. This tragic history has challenged Iraqi writers and makers of culture who try to grapple with its enormity.

Youssef is undoubtedly the most important living Iraqi intellectual and one of the country's greatest modern poets. From his exile in the suburbs of London, his responses have varied from angry political invectives in essay forms attacking the US occupation and its puppets, to tender poems recollecting Iraq's shards from memory and facing what had remained of it. All but three of the poems translated in this collection were written after that catastrophic moment of 2003 and represent this last phase of Youssef's poetry.

While not a nationalist in any traditional sense, many of Youssef's late poems are variations on a central question: what has become of Iraq and how can one confront its reality? His tone varies from wounded anger and defiance as he assumes the collective voice of resistance and protests ("We will not raise our arms") in a poem simply titled "Free Iraqis," to quiet anguish, still in the collective, because "the country we love was finished / before it was born" in the aptly titled "Desperate Poem." At times the tortuous bond to Iraq becomes a burden, as in "Imru' al-Qays' Grandson":

Is it your fault that once you were born in that country?
Three quarters of a century
and you still pay from your ebbing blood
its tax:
(that you were born one day in that country!)

"A Difficult Variation" is at once a poignant performance of the disintegration of Iraq and its erasure, as well as the poet's complex relationship to his homeland. The poem's refrain is the opening line from a memorable poem by another major Iraqi poet, Muhammad Mahdi al-Jawahiri (1900–1997): "Peace be upon Iraq's hills, its two rivers, the bank and the bend, upon the palm trees." But while al-Jawahiri's poem continues with a bucolic description of the Iraqi landscape, Youssef's interrupts the original flow by describing an exilic landscape ("the English hamlet gently dragging its clouds") and the difficulty of representing or imagining al-Jawahiri's Iraq: "can you see the impossible—frond?" The refrain brackets sections depicting a macabre Iraq, but with every refrain, parts of Iraq's landscape are left out so that at the end there is only "Peace be" followed by nothing but the dots Youssef often uses in his poems, as if the Iraq the poet used to recognize has either disappeared or is so disfigured it is unrecognizable.

What compounded Youssef's bitterness was the position taken by a number of Iraqi writers and intellectuals, many of whom were former comrades of Youssef in the Iraqi Communist Party, to support the invasion and war as the only way to overthrow Saddam Hussein's regime and to cooperate with the US and the new regime. Youssef wrote a series of poems that featured the figure of "The Last Communist," a poetic alter ego who embodies the organic oppositional intellectual and poet who will not betray his ideals no matter how the political winds blow. This political faith is beautifully celebrated in "The Last Communist Goes to Heaven." It is in this vein, too, that Youssef uses Pasolini as a mask in "Tonight I Imitate Pasolini" to explore his political otherness and alienation.

Although always Iraqi to the core, Youssef is also an internationalist. He embraces, celebrates, and explores his surroundings wherever life takes him, making or trying to make a home out of exile. The flora and fauna of the English countryside inhabit many of his late poems just as palm trees do. He is also a poet and a citizen of the vast world. His poetic eye peers into New Orleans after it is devastated by Hurricane Katrina to write a poem dedicated to Amiri Baraka. It observes a homeless man in New York speaking to a squirrel, or follows butterflies in Columbia. The poem can serve as that magical space in which Youssef could imagine entering Mecca victorious, hoisting the red flag of an unrepentant communist. It is also the medium for dialogues with Youssef's ancestors and comrades who hail from various epochs and traditions, from Pasolini to the sixth-century pre-Islamic Arab poet Imru' al-Qays. It is very telling that Youssef returns to the figure of Imru' al-Qays in his late poetry and gives one of his last collections the title of the poem included in this translation, "Imru' al-Qays' Grandson." Imru' al-Qays died in exile far away from his home without ever regaining his father's lost kingdom. He was defeated politically, but left an astounding body of poetry. Youssef himself has been on an exilic journey for decades, and he knows that he will not return to Iraq. His arch enemy is the nostalgia that keeps haunting him, as in the title poem, "O Nostalgia: My Enemy":

> I said: the road is long.
> I took out my bread and a piece of cheese from my sack.
> I saw you eyeing me, this way
> sharing my bread and cheese!
> How did you find me?
> Jump at me like a hawk?
> Listen:
> I didn't travel tens of thousands of miles,
> didn't wander across many countries,
> didn't know thousands of branches
> so that you could come now, steal my treasure,
> and corner me.
> Now leave your seat and get off the train,
> my train will speed past after this station
> —so get off,
> and let me go
> where no train will ever stop.

The journey itself, and not its end, is the telos. Armed with more than half a century of experience in writing and in living, Youssef is now freer than ever to go on blurring the line between life and poetry. Writing poetry, after all, is the only thing he has left. "I write so as not to die alone. . . I have no actual life outside poetry," he says.

Youssef believes that poetry is transformative since it captures the ephemeral and the eternal as they embrace. He is a master when it comes to capturing those moments and translating what is

seemingly static into a living poem. Every moment is pregnant with
a potential poem:

> But we,
> the squirrel and I, are trying
> to catch something.

And:

> On the door
> the spider weaves
> what has disappeared:
> it weaves the meaning of the garment . . .

Youssef is, in many ways, what William Carlos Williams was
to the American literary movement in the early part of the last
century—a poet working quietly and unassumingly. He offers
whatever possibility "people find there" (to paraphrase Williams),
in a kind of still life. This is, of course, as much a protest as it
is meditation, for to be still where we are, culturally, denies hu-
manity any improvement.

The new poems in our translation present Youssef's words
in their unique sensitivity—and power—finding English correla-
tives dedicated to the poems' nuances. Youssef's new poems, to an
American reader especially, required the measure of ear that would
pick up the subtle expressions of subject matter—subjects real-
ized through the nuances of Saadi's age and changing events. We
wanted the lines to express the weight of themselves, and this
could only be done with repeated attention to turn of phrase and
emphasis, helping the poem be direct while avoiding confusions or
preciousness from straight translation, a delicate treatment requir-
ing us to approach the individual character of each poem *as well as*
the voice and cadence we know to be Saadi's.

Youssef records, diary-like sometimes, the lines that are human on a scale that has claim to no single century. His new poems are often laments, and they are *offerings* too—often humorous. Emotionally, we know of no other poet writing today whose grip on an endless haze of loss is also a century's witness still capable of comedies and animated exclamations. So, paradoxically, the expressions in these poems are also comforting. Sorrow and despair know their opposites, tauntingly . . . and sometimes wistfully so.

We follow Saadi Youssef's work into a new century. Meditative and resolved, *Nostalgia, My Enemy* is to be prized as both a poet's-poet's book and an "everyman's" (and woman's) book. "Why are the poets silent?" Saadi Youssef asks. Perhaps this book gives them reason to be silent never again.

Sinan Antoon and Peter Money

Nostalgia, My Enemy

Prologue: On Poetry

Is poetry merely a reading of life?

I believe it is deeper and more vast than that.

Humans have numerous ways of reading their life, including science and politics.

But poetry is a different matter.

If science and political struggle promise and prepare for another time, poetry is current, direct and immediate. I mean that poetry's ability to read, participate, and change is more effective and deeper in the veins.

Poetry is transformative.

Poetry transforms in that intimate moment combining the current and the eternal in a wondrous embrace. The tool it uses is the most common, ordinary, and daily one in people's lives. It can be found in the market and on a child's lips before ever being in a book. It is a simple, accessible, and democratic tool. It is the language used by all.

Whence then does poetry bring its miracle?

I believe that there are two deep roots for this miracle.

First: poetry takes language back to its primitiveness when the word was delicate like a taut string—and hence the relationship.

Second: poetry offers the first step on the stairway that carries humans to the heavens—and hence its seduction. As for me, I say: I have no actual life outside poetry.

Poetry is my daily bread and I want it to be the bread of all people.

Undead Nature

Abu al-Khaseeb passes

blue

like morning fog,

a wooden bridge dripping dampness,

there are palm trees

and hyacinths.

The tenderness of happiness

is in the sky.

I will ask about you, son,

when things are cloudy;

I ask about you.

I ask about you.

But I already see you now:

day after day,

night after night.

So wait for me, O son,

we will meet

where the fog is blue

in the morning.

Still Life

The houseplant bends in the heavy air

on the table,

between a full ashtray and the tobacco pouch,

there are gas and electricity bills.

The ship sets sail on the wall,

the bird pecks at the singer's head on a CD cover,

my room is sick of me!

It narrows.

The ship has disappeared.

Night sits in the corner

covering itself with the thick air.

London, 1-2-2004

A Difficult Variation

Peace be upon Iraq's hills, its two rivers, the bank and the bend,

upon the palm trees

and the English hamlet gently dragging its clouds;

evening is close by,

it warms up as it sleeps, like a cat

warding off nightmares from trees drowning in lakes,

evening comes,

slowly and orderly

(you will count its seconds, once)

—will you shut your eyes?

At the end of that hallway

from the window's hill

a chestnut rises

outside the window.

Evening comes

slowly.

It crawls singing a lullaby to your eyelids;

can you see the impossible—frond?

Peace be upon Iraq's hills, its two rivers, the bank, and the bend.

Did I know that my face would be wandering these roads after you?

I left shut doors and a house inhabited by the wind,

your green waters were not my basin,

you left me in the desert fort.

What would I expect of you at night

when you let me down in the morning?

You took to the trenches and said: war is more beautiful,

you shall never see my feet again.

I will seek the roads and taverns,

I am the blind poet.

The frowning autumn gives music for colors—

sunset gives me the opulence of roses

and I ask about you. I ask about you

but as a stung man does after something has afflicted his blood.

Peace be . . .

—I do not want you to reply.

Bid farewell to little that remains,

and peace be upon Iraq's highlands,

slaughtered at the feast,

Baghdad on feast,

teahouses full of bitter tea,

hotels and their distant inhabitants . . .

Prayer is held,

plates are full of bone

soup and lizard meat,

the lands of the mosques are usurped,

their gates open to soldiers, infantry, navy and flying angels

. . .

Peace be . . .

8-31-2003

O Nostalgia: My Enemy

We've been at it for thirty years.

We meet like two thieves on a journey

whose details are not fully known.

With every passing station

the train cars decrease in number,

the light grows dimmer.

But your wooden seat, occupying all trains,

still has its constants.

The etchings of years—

chalk drawings,

cameras no one remembers,

faces

and trees that lie under dirt;

I took a look at you

for a moment,

then rushed panting to the last car

far away from you.

. . .

I said: the road is long.

I took out my bread and a piece of cheese from my sack.

I saw you eyeing me, this way

sharing my bread and cheese!

How did you find me?

Jump at me like a hawk?

Listen:

I didn't travel tens of thousands of miles,

didn't wander across many countries,

didn't know thousands of branches

so that you could come now, steal my treasure,

and corner me.

Now leave your seat and get off the train,

my train will speed past after this station

—so get off,

and let me go

where no train will ever stop.

11-12-2003

The Pagan's Prayer

FOR ABDELRAHMAN MUNIF

O God of the river, praise be to you.

Grant me the bounty of entering the water

my blood has dried up;

I am dried: my shirt is sand, my lips are wood.

Give me, O God of the river, this river's garments.

Thanks be, to you.

Praise be, to you.

For who else do I have, other than you, knower of the water's

secret?

. . .

O God of the Birds, praise be to you too.

Allow me to read the bird's wings in your hands.

Grant me the bounty of sensing the pulse of his forefathers

and to enter.

I have been tied for years to this rock, O God of the Birds!

I crawl

and see each of your creations rising toward you upon wings

—except me.

Grant me, O God of the Birds, two wings!

Praise be.

. . .

O God of the Palms, praise be to you.

Grant me, O god of the Palms, your approval and forgiveness.

I see frames and statures around me becoming shorter:

hunched backs,

those who walked on feet are crawling snakes!

O God of the Palms, approval and forgiveness.

Do not leave me in this plight.

I beseech you! Grant me, O God of the Palms,

the figure of a palm tree.

1-26-2004

The Concerns of a Man, 2000 BC

Night came quickly today.

They say it is because the season has changed

(the priest knows this!)

but I don't know.

Things will not be that different:

the bowl of liquid bread in the tavern,

the night guards at the first turn after the tavern,

and the girl,

she will let me into her chamber

when she waves the oil lamp from the window.

I did not mean to discuss what is not different today.

So please forgive me.

I was trying to ask, in secret (you are a friend):

Why are the poets silent?

Where have they gone?

I no longer see them at the tavern

extemporizing and clamoring.

It is true that invaders have entered Sumer,

that the temple will change the old statues for new ones,

and the scribe's houses have new scribes,

etc. . . .

But where are the poets?

It is said (I don't believe it) that many are now extemporizing

poems in praise of evil merchants,

and that officers of the Akkadian garrison are . . .

well, the night is strange.

Sorry,

the oil lamp glimmers in the window.

Sorry.

London, 4-29-2004

The Evening the Game Was Over

In the silence of some evening

when the forest, too, will disappear in the dark

you will part company with this game

forever!

Years pass by in the glass of the window.

Decades,

creeds—

remembrance of scenes.

You will be happy for a few moments,

you will be light, carried on a carpet

of the first swan's down;

you will be the first child

snuggling a cloud,

snuggling the universe

—leaving this game forever.

London, 9-5-2004

Don't Say

When you sit alone in the garden,

when you approach the harbor,

when you sip a glass of beer in a hurry,

when you go to the market square where the birds are,

when you listen to a song

and fountains are flowing,

when you approach a homeless man in the depth of the night,

when trash piles up,

when streets narrow,

when the singer sleeps through noon,

when sorrow—

when you take a cab today to the airport,

do not, quietly, say good-bye.

Don't say anything

to the country that bequeathed madness to you,

the country that demolished a homeland over your head

and hired death squads

and uprooted the meaning of branches

from your garden—

New York, 8-29-2007

A Neighbor

The retired soldier

(—almost disabled)

lies down every morning in his easy chair

outside his house door

to breathe a bit of the orchard's fragrance

and enjoy the sun.

His wife sits too,

leafing through days, magazines, and bills.

~

The retired soldier

(—almost disabled)

used to shut his eyes a bit,

leaving this chair,

this house,

and his wife too,

to walk through the forests of Indochina

in a minefield.

~

The next will

surely explode

one of these days.

London, 7-19-2007

The Barbarians' Village

They opened their bank in the heart of the village

like a fort in the market—

they raised their walls higher than the stars,

flew with iron horses to guard

the bank at night

—then they said: let's have a banquet,

let's eat a pig's skin!

Drink a bull's blood

and wear buffalo wool!

It was a noisy evening

(every evening is noisy in this village),

people are drunk,

asleep,

as soldiers slip their meat into barracks.

. . .

The guitars will not play.

The saint won't come.

Nor will the nightingale.

There will be no difference whatsoever

between night and day,

taking a village.

I Saw My Father

I was walking

with my father

through a palm grove,

I was light

like a feather,

my father was light,

he was a cloud

and in the cotton of the cloud

I shut (just as in the dream)

my father's eyes.

London, 7-2-2002

Cloves

Where is the scent of cloves coming from?

her hair?

armpit?

or her dress

thrown on the Tunisian rug?

From the third step in the house?

Layla

makes everything smell of cloves.

Layla

is the orchard when it's wet.

She is

what the orchard breathes

when it's watered at night.

Layla knows now

that I am drunk with the scent of cloves,

she stitches together my clouds

and then scatters them together

in a sky like a sheet

as she clasps me.

Layla

feels that my fingers are numb,

over the dunes she knows

my pulse is hers,

my water is hers.

Layla

leaves me sleeping,

rocking between clouds

and cloves.

London, 12-20-2002

Making Love

Like me

you have no desire

for speech to go on too long,

you come to bed

with the splendor of ancient queens

towering,

then you throw your crown

so that gold covers the white sheet,

the bird opens its beak.

. . .

A single drop of dew

and marble

softens.

London, 7-19-2007

Tonight I Imitate Pasolini

You are not the "mystic."

You are not the "surrealist."

You are not one to regret what you loved:

palm trees and your red flag.

You don't beg yellow newspapers for current events

(so now you call *all* newspapers yellow?).

How, then, will you go through this valley of wolves?

Who will translate your poems into EU languages?

Who will nominate you, tonight, at the restaurant, for this

    German or that Croatian prize?

Who writes down your address, phone, and email

adding it to the list of VIPs from all over the world?

Which woman will caress a lock of your white hair from an eye

    in her mobile phone?

—The iron gate will be locked in your face,

and noon will be as severe as night,

it seems that you have known this for a while,

is that why you invited me to the bar today?

Listen please!

I am like you, I feel at home in the Irish pub

(and like you, I do not know how to stop

like Trotsky's trains in the October Revolution) . . .

I told you many times: look out, the world cannot be read like a

   palm anymore!

Yet you are still taken by what I thought you would no more want:

for example, an Iraq resting in a corner of mythology and

   Communists!

Then I believe: you are not the mystic,

you are not the surrealist,

and you are not one to regret what you loved:

palm trees and your red, red flag.

   London, 5-28-2004

The Sun That Never Comes

On this Sunday, tied to the mountain slope,

I miss my country

where summer is already rattling what's left

and the sun aims its rays even in the shade

(the palms are without shades).

On this Sunday, wet like a shepherd's dog,

I miss my country.

All morning I've been saying: I miss my country.

The bones are weary

and my hair is hoary.

On this quiet Sunday I miss my country.

I spent my morning at the square and the café

mumbling a late prayer by the mountainous river

shivering,

—the cold penetrates my blood

with needles of ice.

On this sullen Sunday, I miss my country.

—I never realized until now,

by the village cemetery,

that I am a wretched man

with no country!

Italy, 4-13-2008

Free Iraqis

We will not raise our arms in the square

even if we carry no arms!

We are the descendants of the snake of first water!

We are the descendants of those who worshipped winged bulls!

We are the descendants of those who worshipped fires in snowy

   summits!

And we only raised our arms to the One

when we gave Him our prophecy.

We are the descendants of those who rejected the Romans'

   chariots!

And we're not extinct!

We will not raise our arms in the square,

We will not raise our arms in the square,

We will not raise our arms!

   London, 4-15-2004

I Will Wait

I did not find a bird on a branch

nor a bee on a flower.

I said: today the universe did not wake up to itself!

And this river—

surging,

sloping,

charging like a bull—

will it ever quiet so we can pick up the shells at the bottom

and hear a mermaid's song?

. . .

Carefully I listen:

a bird is calling.

Who is it calling?

Morning has yet to open its window to the hotel.

And this black mountain wraps itself

in raven's feathers.

Posta Reifer Hotel, 4-14-2008

A Secret Entrance to Fortezza

For the workers who make the fort a museum for children and poets:

Stiegl beer,

Marlboro cigarettes,

the blackened boulders transported by Wipptaler Mercedes trucks,

and the dirty waters the Asarco River pushes to the granite walls.

As for the tiny fortified church at the entrance,

the workers have prepared it prematurely

so that others would pray in it . . .

～

The fortress is not far from Posta Reifer Hotel,

just as the fortress is not far from the gold.

Burgomaster Josef Wild, owner of Posta Reifer Hotel,

has the third key to the golden gate—

together with the Nazi commanding officer of the fort

and the representative of the Bank of Italy.

～

At night, the fast trains mix with the rain as they roar.

At night the trees are different,

they become a house,

or smoke.

Then the officers conspire:

Fortezza will be a loophole for rifles

or a fold for canons.

Tsars and scoundrels will come.

I will be a prison suffocating prisoners in steel rings

and a dam against singing.

~

The Russian prisoners of war . . .

I hear them in the night rain,

I hear the sound of their hammers

and shovels . . .

The Russian prisoners of war were digging a tunnel

in the hardened heart of the mountain,

and graves without tombstones—

I hear their wailing.

~

Paris's tricolor flag,

an army of barefoot vagabonds

is knocking at the world's gates;

it was knocking with a fist of blood and songs

and the world's Tsars were shaking . . .

~

The Italian police kept an eye on Licio Gelli for years. They searched his home time and again. But this time, they did not search the safe. They looked in the balcony inside the flowerpots. Amid the begonias and geraniums, Gelli's favorite flowers in his youthful days, they found 162 kilograms of pure gold in one-kilo bars, 40 blocks of silver with CCCP (The Union of Soviet Socialist Republics) etched on them. That took place in 1998.

~

Licio Gelli was a top secret agent to Mussolini and the Gestapo, and it seems that he worked for the communists. He was a banker, journalist, writer, and a poet who garnered many important prizes. But his greater fame was his presiding over the Freemason Assembly known as P-2, which included some of the most famous statesmen, politicians, officers, and businessmen. This gave him secret power to control political events in the fifty years following World War II.

~

Fortezza

was collapsing little by little

over the heads of Tsars . . .

soldiers,

brokers,

and professional arms thieves . . .

Fortezza

is being built again under a second sky

declaring that the world is more beautiful without forts

(even if that fortress is Fortezza) . . .

Posta Reifer Hotel, 4-15-2008

The Night of the Icy Lake

Mountain over mountain and there is a churn:

water like no other water,

trees, but more like rocks,

as if there is a volcano, frozen thousands of years ago.

The sun is cold

and one bird will come,

a bird that will carry us

and our dead

to the gates of Hell.

Fortezza, 4-12-2008

The Glance

Our loss is not the earth

for the earth will stay,

it stayed before us,

it will stay after us,

earth of the singers,

and of silent ones,

earth of those who stay

and transients,

it is the earth of those

who became earth's body.

. . .

What we have lost is not the earth.

The loss is that glance we no longer exchange,

between one child and another

as they share a loaf of bread.

Paris, 10-6-2007

Nature

October,

Paris,

trees shower dusty sidewalks

with gold.

The wind eases a bit,

flows with gold.

Forests are letters,

an airmail

from a countryside

stating: I am the forgotten one,

I live here,

my house is of gold

and dust . . .

Paris, 10-5-2007

The Days

I weaved the dream so often:

I enter mountainous Mecca at dawn

raising my banner (which has been postponed for eons):

a red rag—the barricade flag.

. . .

I will enter mountainous Mecca:

but what will I do there?

Shall I carry the old stone to Manama as the Qarmatians did?

But the road to Manama is not open,

there are no more Qarmatians in Manama.

Shall I fire catapults as al-Hajjaj did in the days of al-Zubayr?

I would be a fool!

The sacred house is nowadays guarded by paratroopers

(Paris-trained!).

The mountains surround—

people will awaken, heavy, and pray the dawn prayers;

they will see me in my jeans and boots

looking mad and disheveled after a long night's journey . . .

Who knows?

Will one of them shout:

"He's a Communist, and must be killed at once!"

London, 6-1-2009

No Play

For whom do I write now?

I have nothing to do with Iraq, nor the capitals.

I have nothing to do with cold friendships

or the women who abandoned me.

I have nothing to do with rifles or raiding fighter jets.

I have nothing to do with gyms.

I have nothing to do with presidential elections

or banks!

I have nothing to do with today's headlines.

I have nothing to do with the food I eat

or the shirt I wore yesterday.

I have nothing to do with the mail.

Or the iron that might weaken iron.

And I have nothing to do with the book, or its people.

For whom do I write now?

I write so as not to die alone.

London, 3-25-2008

Four Sections on Place

I live in Hairfield Hills,

far from London,

closer to my night.

I live in a forest of trees

whose names I don't know

just as I don't know myself.

But I struggle every morning

to know them

by touch.

I live by a lake of forbidden water,

water known to putrid fish

and birds,

water across a fence of trees and rusting iron

—but I will begin

for the sake of this forbidden water.

I will live in a shell of cement and silk

and I say:

it is the shield.

But every evening

I rise to the North Star

and call.

London, 6-2-2008

Fulfillment

I used to,

I often used to hope

as autumn painted forests with gold,

walnut brown,

or muted crimson,

I so hoped to see Iraq's face in the morning

to loosen water's braids over me,

to satisfy its mermaids with salty tears,

to float over Abu al-Khaseeb's rivulets to ask the trees:

do you, trees, know where my father's grave is?

. . .

I often used to hope!

Let it be.

Let autumn finish its cycle.

Iraq's trees will remain naked.

Iraq's trees will remain high.

Iraq's trees will be secretly in the company

of my father's face.

London, 5-21-2003

Observing

On my house door

the spider weaves

his naked clothes

for the air to pass through.

Scents,

summer,

and light pass through

as if the sky is a beginning—

. . .

On the door

the spider weaves

what has disappeared:

it weaves the meaning of the garment . . .

London, 7-28-2009

Seasons (4)

All day, the white blossoms of the climbing plant

fall on the second-floor walkway:

these piled white blossoms

glisten as they wither

like the dust of stars falling all night—

I try not to step on them,

I lighten my burden as I walk

in vain:

even when withered, they turn

to catch me,

take me from the sole of my feet,

reach my hair

scattering and shining over my wool shirt—

. . .

Tonight the blossoms came to me in my dream

to take me with them—

I shall be happy!

London, 9-2-2002

Conversation

As fall winds wailed

in the surrounding hills

he said:

are we, my friend, two rocks?

How often have the winds wailed?

How often have we been struck

—by cold and harm?

How often have we lost our bets?

Yet we stand here.

. . .

I said: don't grieve.

We are the eye of time.

London, 6-27-2009

Hamlet's Balcony

I am in the watchtower now:

the wind enters the sea,

the sea enters the wind,

the horizon is salt.

Even ships, at this frowning port, seem confounded.

The morning I hope for

is not in Denmark.

Evening will come

and as night falls

an owl, more eerie than the castle ditch,

will caw—

The royal feast is tonight.

. . .

Let me celebrate:

To be yourself or not to be

and then madness will come

. . .

The Balcony of the Poor House

Paint

was peeling off its white clothes on the ceiling

quietly and calmly

casting them off like old money notes

into the flower pots

or on the head of the one

gazing on the balcony.

The morning is humid

and this ever-falling paint

has reached the garden below,

even the shoes of the one

gazing on the balcony

and the air he is breathing.

. . .

He will shake off what has fallen on his shirt,

his head—

perhaps his hand will even reach down to his shoes.

But the morning song,

the song of a lifetime,

is still burdened with scattered paint.

London, 7-2-2002

Andes Butterflies

I am waiting for what night erases:

blueness has already disappeared,

I only see a bird

whose eternal home is my brick roof . . .

I will light a lamp,

attempt an open space for me where paths entwine.

The peak is white,

red trees on the slopes . . .

I drink a Cuba Libre,

a few droplets of a summer rain yet to fall

surprise my eyelashes—

I open my eyes as wide as the world:

there are black butterflies

enormous

like bush birds

fluttering across the hotel toward the slope,

. . .

The country house

out here in the white suburb

loses all its maps

and floats.

London, 6-15-2004

An Abandoned Shore

A boat,

two thirds on the shore,

keeps rolling—.

The sea shrivels,

seeking refuge from the ropes of rain

—in its own density.

A boat,

which will not rise

at dawn like me,

to start

its fishing journey.

London, 12-21-2003

Imru' al-Qays' Grandson

Is it your fault that once you were born in that country?

Three quarters of a century

and you still pay from your ebbing blood

its tax:

(that you were born one day in that country!)

and what is it?

You know its mountains and valleys,

false histories,

its cityless cities,

villages where there is nothing—

that utter darkness . . .

and you know that the country where you were born

did not breathe the meaning of country.

. . .

The question is: what is it to you

now when you are asked to do the impossible?

London, 5-22-2005

Mustafa the Egyptian

He has the prophet's name and features.

He has a wooden box:

his rag, brushes, and paint,

and the neighborhood street.

All the cafés are his:

the tables

—even the sidewalk of the municipality by the coast is his!

The tourists and what they wear on their feet,

the soldiers,

and those who come by ferry are all his.

. . .

The morning is now almost forenoon.

The breeze carrying the Nile to the city warms up.

Thick dust covers the glass of the neighborhood café.

The tea has settled in the cup.

I said to him: Mustafa!

You have been polishing shoes since the morning . . .

do you go to school?

. . .

Mustafa cannot read:

he polishes people's shoes—

this orphan prophet!

London, 2-16-2008

Rock-Solid Time

From now on you will enter a more solid shell,

a shell that gets wet

at the first dawn to thirst all day.

Hours are lines,

years are circles,

and history is this moment.

. . .

Are you happy?

Are you miserable?

Do you wish to get out of this shell?

The dream-shell,

the fort-shell,

the shell besieging your shirt like a lead garment?

. . .

Fine!

What will you do at the end of the night

when screams penetrate the shell's walls,

screams of joy—

the screams of wild ducks?

London, 9-23-2006

The Homeless Man and the Squirrel

Saturday morning was ecstatic:

a tepid sun,

a breeze carrying the scent of grass

and the beginnings of cold;

the fence around Washington Square Park was wet.

. . .

The homeless man shook off his blanket

and folded it.

He took out a piece of bread

from the pocket of his jeans,

looked around

and waited by the cypress tree.

The squirrel came down,

inched closer

until it almost touched his palm.

It picked up the crumbs

and danced like a bird.

The homeless man

went on

speaking the squirrel's language

like a prophet.

New York, 8-18-2007

Chess

Old inmates,

blacks unemployed for a century and a half,

professors who've abandoned sacred university seats

and took ones on the sidewalk,

women who are tired of the play,

the roles of Adam & Eve.

Night revelers who lost their way home—

. . .

In every square there is a board!

New York, 8-9-2007

Light Hallucination

Because the rain

is sluggish,

since you came to live on the hill in the suburb,

permanent and visible

like the garden gate or house door—

like tree trunks,

you daydream of the rain—

rain forming from a flower scattered in the mist,

rain of enormous drops,

rain of waves covering the shirts of lost seamen,

the tropical rain of mercy in a hurricane,

rain you cannot hear:

rain of locusts,

rain in the roots of the country,

rain of ashes.

6-1-2006

The Irish Rose

The Irish Rose does not produce blossoms

as we know or read about.

I have one here in a corner of my orchard—

(let's call these four yards an orchard, I have nothing to lose).

I have had it since I arrived three years ago to this faraway place,

I tend to it,

water it

(every evening, she said)

—waiting for blossoms,

or for a promise of a blossom.

(It is called *Jumbudh* in Basra.)

Failure!

Failure,

people here say.

An Irish Rose can think

it is in London . . .

An Irish Rose,

how will it be in Basra, then?

How in London, and not in Dublin?

10-10-2004

New Orleans

TO AMIRI BARAKA

Sleep, oh, sleep.

Sleep, oh, sleep.

I'm sleeping,

we are both sleeping,

in a bed of water.

Sleep, oh, sleep . . .

Water might become fire, winds: axes.

We are not at the doomsday's dawn, humble and thirsty,

nor are we the first to be in chains.

No graves were sundered in the wilderness,

nor slave ships appear on the horizon.

As if cotton melting from an enormous black nut

has penetrated the veins of stone and asphalt,

we are the scum of the earth and the cities that we built.

Swamps are calling us with names we thought had been forgotten,

with time and that distant war two centuries ago . . .

The stars are our gravestones in the water.

The engulfing silence is our prayer.

There is music in the distance.

So it's Black Africa.

Sleep, oh, sleep.

Sleep, oh, sleep.

I'm sleeping,

we are both sleeping,

in a bed of water.

I will light a lantern for the blind singer

and two for the barefoot women walking on embers.

We go along with maps, with those forlorn by time.

(Perhaps we will reach the land that never was?)

Is it Africa? Green, green . . .

Master, you who said: you are the salt of this earth!

Naked are the lies,

we are finished with this whore!

Now the road is paved with pus and vomit

and drunkards (who aren't drunk!),

we shall fold that page;

if today isn't our beginning, then when will we begin?

We will be satisfied by the return of all the ships.

The bridges are all on fire,

water is fire.

Sleep, oh, sleep.

Sleep, oh, sleep.

I'm sleeping,

we are both sleeping,

in a bed of water.

Sleep, oh, sleep.

Sleep, oh, sleep.

Like buffaloes, those iron birds headed northward, in full speed

to every place and spot.

They left us nothing but shadows,

our blackness isn't darker than the under-skin of a crowned white man.

Let us see your magic!

What is safety for iron birds is the imminent separation of two

    nations for us—

time was lulled by a song of ours,

silk was built by what the piano weaved.

—The drum is beating!

Dum, dum, dum, dum.

The drum is beating!

Dum, dum, dum, dum.

The drum is beating!

. . .

Don't sleep!

London, 5-9-2005

The Wretched of the Heavens

We will go to God

naked.

Our shroud is our blood,

our camphor:

the teeth of dogs

turned wolves.

The closed cell suddenly swung open

for the female soldier to come.

Our swollen eyes could not make her out,

perhaps because she comes from a mysterious world,

she did not say a thing;

she was dragging my brother's bloody body behind her,

like a worn-out mat.

We will walk to God

barefoot:

our feet lacerated,

our limbs wounded.

Are Americans Christians?

We have nothing in the cell to wipe the lying body,

only our blood

congealing in our blood

—and this smell coming from the continent of slaughterhouses

. . . Angels will not come here,

the air is perturbed,

these are the wings of hell's bats,

the air is motionless.

We have been waiting for you, O Lord.

Our cells were open yesterday.

We were lifeless on their floor,

and you did not come, O Lord.

But we are on the way to you.

We will remain on the way even if you let us down.

We are your dead sons and have declared our resurrection.

Tell your prophets to open the gates of cells and paradises!

Tell them that we are coming!

We have wiped our faces and hands with clean earth.

The angels know us one by one.

London, 5-10-2004

December

I will not open my window:

even the grass is drowning in the sea winds;

trees are shaking under the rain.

The room is still (the house has double-windows);

I hear the clock ticking:

tick

tick tick tick,

I can hear the pond's tiny waves in the distance.

Nearby: tiny waves of fingers . . .

Is my lover back after a long trip?

The yellow flowers at the entrance are very early.

No visitor knocks at my door.

Even the birds found a shelter.

But we,

the squirrel and I, are trying

to catch something.

London, 12-20-2003

The Last Communist Goes to Heaven

Sunday night, the last Communist was insomniac. His girlfriend had left Paris at noon. Minute after minute, light rain was falling heavier. The Australian wine he had been gulping in large glasses almost threw him down. Then his car battery was dead.

Things have settled down; so what is he to do now?

The last Communist went scavenging in the top shelves. There is dust on the old books. Cobwebs, the remains of a bee's wings. But he snatched the book and read:

Our situation is astounding.

An angel came to accompany the last Communist to heaven.

He said: I have roamed the seven horizons in search of a pure human. The people I saw were wondrous, praying and all. But I was seeking two traits: purity and justness. The heavens are open, so let's take off so you can be in paradise in a minute!

The last Communist was on the couch. Breathing calmly and smiling, as if the perfumes of paradise were truly overflowing his nocturnal palace . . .

London, 6-28-2006

Bees Visit Me

A bee perched on my shirt,

then another.

Blossoms were radiant,

shaking the beechnut tree

and the orchard——.

How did the bees come?

My table doesn't have much:

a piece of bread and cheese,

but it overflows with French wine . . .

Is that what the bees are after?

What is strange is that they cling to my shirt,

persistent.

Do they know that honey,

the universe,

and the end

are under the shirt?

——That pollen is quivering?

London, 8-8-2009

Heavy Time

Everything now quiets down:

the jazz songs on the radio,

trees in the nearby forest,

silver fish at the bottom

and that woman/cat on the phone.

Will this pale, calm as death, Sunday evening bring the trumpet?

Are the ceiling tiles a cymbal waiting for the strike?

Or is the spider's web both the rope and the dock?

Dry air slips in between the door and the hallway,

from nowhere a bird flutters.

One note descends.

One star.

Evening by the Lake

Yesterday

by the lake

the rain was warm,

soft,

like your skin after a dip in the sea.

I though of you a bit

and swore right away:

I have to catch the evening train!

But I'm lazy,

as you know,

so I forgot about the train—

thought of you a lot,

and brought my face closer

to the surface of the water,

to watch how the sky's waters go home,

how this evening is born.

A Desperate Poem

The country we love was finished

before it was even born.

The country we did not love has claimed

the blood left in our veins.

We were its people,

say: yes, but a blaze

took us on from birth.

Were we asleep,

or unaware?

Were our boats weaving the cane into a noose?

Were the birds from Hell?

I have no more dust

to vanish as it falls from my fingers.

Time is still.

. . .

The country we love is finished.

London, 11-17-2007

A Fawn behind the Fence

The winds wailed in the evening.

There was a cloud over the lake's waters,

but a surprising sun appeared

on the distant horizon

red.

I hadn't seen the sun during the day . . .

Has the world changed?

The day is blind,

and night is opening its eyelids.

. . .

I wish you were here next to me.

Just now a fawn was behind the fence.

I watched it

feasting on thin leaves,

I watched it

pulling branches

then releasing them,

to fall on their faces.

A Spring Downpour

Water,

tens of thousands of threads

knotting their ladder

between towering tree tops and the walkway;

the wind is favorable.

White flowers fly in the wind:

I gather snow in my palm

and enter my own house to scatter it

on the silence of my sheets,

onto my corner pillow.

The snow's melt cannot become tears,

I know, of course—these white flowers will wither,

soon I know the wind quiets down,

this sun becomes summer sun,

and I will travel to a country I don't know.

But what is the world to me?

This moment is enough.

This white moment

white.

London, 4-30-2004

Listening

Every now and then

(read: every other *year!*)

I listen to my heart beating

(do you take what I say to be playing? speaking too figuratively?),

I said: I try to make sure that my heart is beating,

and listen carefully:

I sit and relax,

the windows, shut tight,

no car engines roaring,

no winds,

no rain wallowing over the doubled glass.

I shut my lids,

relax my arm

and listen:

Did it beat?

Did it beat?

Did it beat?

I lower my head to the left,

my chin touching the new shirt I bought only yesterday,

O heart!

O heart!

What kind of companions are we really?

You speak to me once a year and I greet you back.

Speech.

Postponed life,

now I hear your voice

beating,

bugles,

a night cavalry advancing in the expanse,

or trumpeting the day of resurrection?

Notes

Undead Nature

Abu al-Khaseeb: A river and a city in southern Iraq where Youssef was born. His son, Haydar, died of a heart attack in Japan at the age of thirty.

A Difficult Variation

"Peace be upon Iraq's hills, its two rivers, the bank and the bend, upon the palm trees." This line, which is repeated throughout the poem and is gradually truncated until the final "Peace be" with nothing after it, is a famous line from a memorable poem by Muhammad Mahdi al-Jawahiri (1900–1997). Al-Jawahiri was one of Iraq's and the Arab world's great poets who had to live in exile because of his political views and opposition to dictatorship.

The Pagan's Prayer

Abdelrahman Munif (1933–2004): A Saudi writer and intellectual, considered one of the most important Arab novelists of the twentieth century. His political outspokenness caused him to live in exile most of his life.

Tonight I Imitate Pasolini

Pier Paolo Pasolini (1922–1975) was an Italian poet, film director, and intellectual.

A Secret Entrance to Fortezza

Fortezza (fortress) was built in the 1830s by the Hapsburg Empire on one of Europe's most important travel routes to defend the passage. However, the fortress never witnessed any battles. In 2008, Youssef was one of a number of writers and artists who were invited to critically reflect on this place and its history and imagine various scenarios. He wrote a series of eight poems.

The Days

Qarmatians: A ninth-century Islamic offshoot group which established a utopian republic based on egalitarianism and shared property. They had attacked Mecca and taken its sacred black stone with them to Manama. They were defeated in 967 CE.

Al-Hajjaj: A seventh-to-eighth-century, notoriously brutal governor of Iraq who attacked Mecca with catapults to settle a civil war.

Imru' al-Qays' Grandson

Imru' al-Qays: A sixth-century pre-Islamic poet and the author of the first *mu'allaqa* (Arabian Ode). He is an iconic figure in the history of Arabic poetry. He died in exile after failing to regain his father's lost kingdom.

Mustafa the Egyptian

Mustafa, "chosen" in Arabic, is one of the names of the Prophet Muhammad, who was himself an orphan.

The Irish Rose

Basra: A city in southern Iraq, close to Youssef's hometown.

The Wretched of the Heavens

This poem was written following the Abu Ghraib scandal. In "We have wiped our faces and hands with clean earth," Youssef uses a particular verb (*tayammamna*) with important resonance. In the Islamic tradition, *"tayammum"* is using clean earth for ablutions and purifications if and when water is not available. The sentence appears in the Qur'an a few times, but as a form of a command: "[If]. . you do not find water, then use some clean earth and wipe your faces and hands." See *The Qur'an: A New Translation*, tr. Tarif Khalidi. (London: Penguin Books, 2009). See verses 4:43 and 5:6.

SAADI YOUSSEF is one of the pioneers of modern Arabic poetry. He was born in Abu al-Khaseeb, in southern Iraq, in 1934. He studied Arabic literature in Baghdad and worked as a teacher and journalist. Youssef started writing very early and published his first collection of poems in 1952. His political engagement and radical opposition to various Iraqi regimes forced him to live in exile in Algeria, Lebanon, Yemen, France, Yugoslavia, Cyprus, Jordan, and Syria. He is one of the most prolific and influential Arab poets of the twentieth century. His oeuvre includes forty-five books of poetry and nine other works of prose. He has translated Whitman, Cavafy, Ritsos, Lorca, Popa, Ungaretti, Ngugi wa Thiong'o, and Wole Soyinka into Arabic. In 2012 he won the prestigious Naguib Mahfouz Prize. Youssef has been living in London since 2000. *Without an Alphabet, Without a Face: Selected Poems of Saadi Youssef* (translated by Khaled Mattawa) was published by Graywolf Press in 2002.

SINAN ANTOON is an Iraqi-born poet and novelist. He has published two collection of poetry in Arabic, *A Prism; Wet with Wars* and *One Night in All Cities*, and one collection in English, *The Baghdad Blues*. His novels include *The Pomegranate Alone* and *I`jaam: An Iraqi Rhapsody,* which was translated into five languages. He translated Mahmoud Darwish's last prose book, *In the Presence of Absence.* He is co-founder and co-editor of *Jadaliyya.* Additionally, Antoon directed the acclaimed documentary *About Baghdad.* He is an associate professor at the Gallatin School, New York University.

PETER MONEY is an American poet. He lives in Vermont and has taught at Lebanon College and the Center for Cartoon Studies, and has been the director of Harbor Mountain Press. His books include *Che: A Novella in Three Parts, To Day—Minutes Only,* and *Finding It: Selected Poems.*

Nostalgia, My Enemy is typeset in Perpetua, designed by English sculptor and typeface designer Eric Gill (1882–1940). Composition by BookMobile Design and Digital Publisher Services, Minneapolis, Minnesota. Manufactured by Versa Press on acid-free 30 percent postconsumer wastepaper.